Donald V. Huard, Ph.D.

Teen-Agers: What Will Cigarettes, Booze, "Safe" Sex, And Drugs Do For You?

Published by 1stBooks 1/13/2012

ISBN: 978-1-5850-0314-3 (sc)

This book is printed on acid free paper.

Printed in the United States of America
Bloomington, IN

Synopsis

It would be a mistake to assume that most teen-agers smoke or that they are involved in drug abuse, are constrained by the chains of alcoholism or that they are engaging in premarital sex. Yet, every teen-ager is faced from time to time with temptations that put him or her in a quandary over these things.

You can't get to any kind of positive grown-up life-style by routinely escaping into self-centered play. Sooner or later, anyone who elects to avoid reality by spending too much of life playing and too little of life setting up good goals and working like hell to achieve them gets left behind by others.

It's very sad when young people waste the potential that they have. But, there is a brighter side to this. One of the truly great things about America is that most of its teen-agers have their heads on straight

That's right, most of today's young people are reasonably well-balanced and their heads are squarely on their shoulders. Most kids have straight edges...

To A.J., Lindsay, Lauren, Tyler, Jeremy,

Stacia, Becky, Derek, Ann,

Bobby Dean, Cortney,

Nathan, Dylan and Hannah

as they struggle with their teens...

Also by Donald V. Huard, Ph.D.

Behavioral Statistics: An Introduction to the Basic Methods of Analysis and Persuasion **ISBN 0-8403-7408-9**

Teen-agers: What Will Cigarettes, Booze and Drugs Do for You? **ISBN 0-9661606-1-4**

Teen-agers: "Safe" Sex Isn't, But Abstinence Is...**ISBN 0-9661606-2-2**

Contents

Chapter One

What will Cigarettes do for you?

Your friends smoke. Why shouldn't you smoke? It's cool! It's grown up. If you smoke you're not hurting anyone else. Why can't you decide for yourself? Why are mom and dad always preaching at you about not smoking, especially when *they* smoke?

Are those the questions that you want answered? Or don't you care about those answers? Maybe you just prefer to do as you please, without asking any of those questions, even if it involves risking your health. Maybe you wish mom and dad would always say yes to you, regardless of any dangers that might be present if you do what *you* want.

Maybe you just want to show them that you can't be controlled all of the time, especially now that you have grown up. You' re sick of being told what you can and cannot do.

Mom and dad do tend to treat you as though you're just a kid. That really bugs you sometimes. Why can't they see that you are old enough to think for yourself? Can't they see that you have to make some of your own mistakes, so that you will learn what works and what doesn't?

Mom and dad should be able to see that being young today is a lot harder than it was way back when they were your age. You have the drug problem today and booze and sex and violence and guns on the streets. It was easier for them, not so easy for you. So why do they treat you like you don't know anything ?

Well now, answering all of those questions is going to be quite a chore. Getting any young person to read the answers is also difficult. You see, most kids just don't want the answers to those questions, even though they ask for them.

Most kids just want to do their things, hoping that mom and dad won't get in the way. Most kids just want to do what their friends want them to do. They want the approval of their friends. They hate the idea that they might not be accepted by their friends. They will even defy their parents at times in order to impress their own friends. Lots of kids defy their teachers because it gets them "high fives" from their friends. They meet across from the school grounds, on the other side of the fence, where they can smoke and the teachers can't tell them they can't. Many will smoke cigarettes, smoke pot or sniff a little of this or that in order to impress their friends.

But now, wait a minute... Maybe you aren't one who always goes along with the other kids. Maybe you like to think things out a bit first, that is, before you leap into a world of trouble. Maybe you are even grown up enough to do a little research about such things as the use of tobacco or marijuana.

Maybe you even have the courage to stand up to your friends and tell them that you' re able to think for yourself. Maybe you are even smart enough to tell them when you think they are doing something gross, something that is harmful. Maybe you aren't the kind of kid who just goes along, regardless.

Of course, it's easier to just go along. It's easier to just avoid reading any book like this one. Not many kids want to investigate the reasons for doing what's smart when it's so much fun to do what their friends are doing, even things their friends might do that are just plain dumb. Like sniffin' glue. Or like sniffin' "chemo" or one of those other cool things that can blow your mind.

Well, maybe you're different. Maybe you are kind of special, the kind of teen-ager who wants to avoid the pitfalls and really wants to grow up with straight edges. Maybe you've got the guts to do what will make your parents proud of you rather than ashamed. Maybe you'll be grown up enough to tell your friends that cigarettes, pot and booze are not for you. Maybe you will read the rest of this little book to get the answers to those questions you've been asking.

Do you think that it would be a good idea to just start smoking the way your friends did and wait to see how it affects you or would it be a good idea to find out what that smoking will do to you before you decide to start? We're not talking here about the long-term effects of smoking on your lungs and your heart. We're talking about what is going to happen to you ***now*** if you start to smoke.

Wouldn't it be a good idea to find out what to expect so that you can make a good decision? That way you could avoid a lot of unpleasantness if you should decide to leave the cigarettes alone.

Cigarettes have nicotine in them. Everyone knows that. The cigarette company executives will tell you that nicotine isn't addictive, but most people know that they are lying through their teeth in order to protect their jobs. You see, if young people don't smoke, then they won't become addicted and cigarette sales will go down and lots of jobs will be lost by people producing and selling tobacco products. You can get snowed real easy by just believing that nicotine is not addictive. Did you know that about ninety percent of all adult smokers began smoking before they were eighteen years old?

Here's how nicotine works on the human body. Your body is much like a car motor that runs smooth and has lots of power if the right mixture of fuel and oxygen is getting into its cylinders. If the wrong mixture gets into the engine, the smooth purr becomes a sputter, the engine chokes and much of the power is lost.

At first, smoke with nicotine in it makes your body choke and sputter. But if you keep smoking, your body is able to adjust to the presence of nicotine and soon it runs fairly smooth. It seems as though no harm is being done. In fact, after a while most smokers can puff away and even inhale the smoke with no problem other than that they smell of cigarettes all of the time (girls who don't smoke hate the smell of boys who do).

Then comes the problem...It sort of sneaks up on you. Once your body is adjusted to nicotine always being in your blood, you have to have it there all of the time just to be comfortable. If you try to stop smoking, you will get the "jitters" and feel shaky and anxious. So you have to light up many times each day just to keep from feeling tense. **<u>You are hooked.</u>** You are addicted to nicotine. It doesn't take long, only a month or two. Many people are hooked for their entire lives.

The effect of nicotine addiction is a very powerful one. Presently, forty-six million people in the United States are under the control of its influence. It's not likely that any of them ever intended to become so dependent on anything when, years earlier, they started smoking to show their independence.

"I just started smoking in middle school," says one seventeen year-old. "Now I'm in high school. I have my own car, but I can't afford gas for it because I have to have cigarettes all of the time. I could be stuck with this stupid habit for the rest of my life." Another teen complains, "A lot of really neat girls won't go out with me because I smell like cigarettes all of the time. I can't blame them. I guess I'm really hooked. Guys who chew tobacco really get disgusted looks from the chicks. They won't go out with them, no how."

When you really think about it, it's very sad. Many teen-agers who think that by smoking they are showing their friends and parents that they are grown up enough to be free to make their own decisions become so hooked on smoking that they are not free at all. They are controlled by their need for nicotine. Some of them will be able to break the habit. Some will never be able to get free again. Before they started smoking, they had no way to know which way it would be for them. Now, is that the pits, or what?

If you start smoking, how will it be for you? Will you be one of those who can quit any time you want? Or will you be spending money on cigarettes for the rest of your life? You have no way to know ahead of time which way it will be for you. Most smokers need a full pack a day. Many need more than that.

Is it smarter to just go ahead and start smoking the way your friends did or is it better to seriously consider what nicotine can do for you and then make your decision? Would you rather be smarter than your friends who smoke or is it better to be just like your friends who already smoke? Do you want to be a grown up person who smokes or one who can get along without cigarettes, one who is really free?

Only you can decide...

Chapter Two

And Then There's Booze...

Later in this book we'll talk about the legal aspects of smoking, smoking pot and using alcohol. But before we do, let's consider the way so many grown-ups use alcohol for fun and the consequences of using too much too often. Too often, people get hooked on cigarettes *and* alcohol. Many of them, in fact, can't live without either of them.

No one who becomes an alcoholic really intends to become dependent on the substance. No one ever said, "I'm going to drink all of the time, more and more until I get to the point that I have to have a drink all of the time." As with the use of cigarettes, there are strings attached that can slowly strengthen into chains. Then those chains become so strong that they cannot be broken. Maybe that's why they talk about chain smokers.

But how does it happen? It's really kind of interesting the way it works. To get a clearer look at the process, why don't we consider what might happen to a drinking teenager, say, someone who is a sophomore or junior in high school.

You would never let that happen to you, of course, but some kids do and it's not difficult to explain how some of them become alcoholics. Alcohol has the ability to reduce anxiety and tension. It's a nice effect. It feels real good, especially for those who tend to be a bit stressed and tense much of the time.

Do you remember how it was pointed out in Chapter One that smokers get accustomed to nicotine in their blood and get those "jitters" if they try to stop smoking? Those "jitters" are not very pleasant and they produce anxiety and discomfort. Do you remember how lighting up another cigarette eases the "jitters" and how that makes the smoker comfortable again? The smoker who is hooked smokes to keep away the discomfort. Of course, he or she enjoys smoking as well because the nicotine keeps a person relaxed.

Psychologists who research this process point to the fact that behaviors that reduce tension are reinforced (strengthened) by a process called *negative reinforcement*. It involves the continued strengthening of any habit that takes away negative or bad feelings, feelings that are unpleasant.

That negative reinforcement process applies to the use of alcohol as well. Let's set up a little scenario that shows how a teen-ager might develop a problem with his (or her) use of alcohol.

Jim is a typical teen-ager (if there is such a thing) who loves to drive a car, go to football games, date the pretty girls and hang around with his buddies. He spends much of his time attending classes at school during the week and some of his time having fun socializing on the busy weekends. If he is a sophomore or a junior in high school, he already has a girlfriend or two and has become much aware that girls are very soft, that they are sweet, smell pretty if they don't smoke and they have all of those good attributes that turn him on. Life is really great if there is someone "special" in Jim's life.

But life is not always rosy. Sometimes he has fights with his girlfriend. Sometimes his car breaks down and he doesn't have the necessary money he needs to fix it. Sometimes things don't go too well at school. His parents are driving him up the wall by all of their preaching and he feels resentful. Sometimes life is the pits. All of that is usual for teen-agers because nobody has it perfect all of the time.

When things are going wrong for one reason or another, because mom and dad don't understand or perhaps because his girlfriend is showing signs of being interested in someone else, Jim feels really pressured to set things right, but he doesn't quite know how to get things altogether. He is uneasy and tense much of the time. He feels like a real "nerd."

It should be pointed out that this is reasonably normal for most high school kids. In fact, just about all teen-agers go through lots of anxiety over all sorts of things much of the time. They struggle with coping. So much of their time is spent in the doldrums. They are moody and unwilling to communicate with anyone, anyone except their closest friends.

Jim and his friends sneak their way into the local nightspots on the weekends to cruise the scene and to check out the cute "chicks." Jim might be a bit tired of his girlfriend Jenny's moodiness and he might actually be considering finding a different "significant other" for himself. After all, a guy gets tired of always wondering where he stands. How much is a guy supposed to take?

The search for someone new poses all sorts of anxiety

and potential threat for Jim. He sees everyone else having a great time, bouncing to the incredibly loud rock and country music (which he can't stand). He's pretty good at premarital "jive" himself. Outwardly, it is a scene of great happiness, with lots of goofin' off, lots of fun. It's cool... Inwardly, however, it is not so great for Jim or for that matter, not so great for his buddies either.

For most young people, the inward feelings experienced while trying to survive on the social scene are characterized by anything *but* relaxed emotional comfort. The building of new relationships, in hopes that one will be lasting and mutually rewarding, involves a considerable amount of anxiety-producing risk. Jim asks himself, "How can I get any girl I'm turned on to, to be turned on by me? What if I fail to impress her," he asks himself when he gets ready to hit on one of the foxier ones? "And what if I say something stupid?"

Jim is anxious because with each venture into the unknown, that is, with each attempt to hit it off with someone new, there is an increase in stress and anxiety that comes from the chance of more disappointing rejection. No one wants to get dissed, including Jim. "You try to be nice, the chick thinks you're a nerd," he complains.

Jim's friends are all trying to handle their own feelings of uneasiness. The girls experience this anxiety as well. They are attracted to certain cool boys, but they wonder if they can trust them. "What if he doesn't like me," she asks? "What if he comes on too fast?"

New relationships tend to be awkward and uneasy for awhile. Sometimes, they are downright painful. Very few of the teen-agers are as confident about themselves and the outcome of the social process as they would like to have their friends believe.

Jim's friends get him some beer to drink. Or maybe he starts with a little vodka. The alcohol in his drink eases his nervousness. He begins slowly to discover that alcohol seems to make his tense inner world feel more tolerable. Alcohol helps break the ice. Therein lies its powerful, personal, persuasive influence, rarely recognized by the user until it gains control over him as it becomes the usual way of coping with life's many pressures.

Do you remember when it was suggested that any behavior that is followed by anxiety reduction is strengthened? Well, that's that negative reinforcement thing again. If that behavior is smoking, the smoking habit forms. It gets very, very strong. If the behavior is social drinking, then the drinking is strengthened by that tension reduction. It could become a dominant conditioned habit pattern for Jim. He could become an alcoholic.

When Jim feels moody and depressed, alcohol will make him feel better. When he lacks confidence, he will get it back if he drinks. That strengthens his desire to continue drinking. He's more relaxed when he is drinking. That also strengthens his need to drink more. His drinking friends encourage him to drink. The "high fives" he gets from them also reinforce his desire to drink. The more he drinks, the more reinforcement he gets. So he continues to drink.

By now, you can see that the trap is closing on Jim. Soon his behavior will tend to change in ways that will find his friends criticizing him for his drinking so much and acting like the nerd he didn't want to be. He isn't the same sweet fellow he used to be. Now all he wants to do is drink. He's no fun to be around unless he thinks he's had enough to drink. By that time, however, he's no longer fun to be around.

Jim's interest in his school work fades. His grades drop. Everyone seems to be down on him, so he drinks more to ease the pressures put on him by his friends and his parents. It becomes a vicious circle. The more he drinks to ease the pressures, the more criticism he gets which puts him under more pressure, so he drinks more, etc., etc...

Is it better to just go ahead and start drinking to see what it does to you or would it be better to learn what it can do to you and then decide whether or not to drink? Of course, you may be someone who can quit any time you want. But some kids just can't. And there's no way to know ahead of time which way it would be for you.

If you drink, it could be "Good-bye, freedom" for you. The alcoholic really is involved in a process that costs him his freedom. He's not free to do his thing without alcohol. Alcohol *becomes* his thing. He tends to endanger others by drinking and driving. He becomes a pitiful slave to his drinking habit. Often, he must be cared for by others because he cannot manage his own life. What starts out as a fun time, living the good life, becomes a life of misery for those who get hooked on alcohol. They tend to lose their friends. They become too defensive about their drinking and rationalize their problem away, suggesting that others drink more than *they* do.

Alcoholics find everyone else to blame for their own problems. They are inclined to make excuses for letting other people down. They become self-centered, unhappy and demanding. Many become verbally abusive and a significant percentage become physically violent toward members of their own families.

The alcoholic won't listen to anyone. He (or she) listens only to the need for more alcohol. Heart and liver damage is an inevitable result of compulsive drinking and the alcoholic is apt to live a shorter life.

It's so sad...

But, what about *you?* Is alcohol for you? Would you rather be smarter than your friends who drink or would you rather drink just like your friends who drink? If you decide to drink, how do you know that you will always be able to keep it at a reasonable level so that you will never lose control? Do you want to risk becoming a grown-up person who drinks or would you rather be one who can get along without alcohol, one who is really free? Only you can decide...

Chapter Three

Smoking Pot... No Problem

Marijuana cigarettes contain a chemical substance called THC which stands for tetra-hydrocannabinol. Everyone knows that. However, did you know that the use of that stuff can be habit forming? Of course, some of your friends and even some doctors will tell you that it isn't addictive. Well, in a purely physical sense and with only limited use it may not be addictive for some people, but in a psychological sense, it can be very habit forming. That habit can actually become so strong that it can result in the domination of some teen-agers' lives.

Some reasonably well-intended people who favor pot smoking fail to make the distinction between addiction and psychological dependence. They think that just because marijuana may not be addictive for some, it won't be habit forming either. However, the habit of smoking pot can get quite strong before you know it. It gets out of control, not because of a heroin-like addiction, but because the desire for the euphoria it produces becomes too enticing to resist. Those who are much inclined to smoke pot for entertainment, find themselves smoking it every chance they get. It's not that they started out by saying, "I'm going to smoke pot all of the time, until I have to have pot all of the time." They just did it enough to get dependent on it. The strings became chains that can't be broken. Attempts to break the habit result in anxiety and depression.

Most of them can quit if they want to, but some can't stop wanting pot. They just go around with their watery eyes and their sniffles and their stinkin' clothes with their reduced interest in doing anything more productive than getting high. Their grades start to drop and they are not interested in doing anything about it (this is called the amotivational syndrome).

You see, just as with alcohol, all you need to develop a strong dependence on *any* psychotropic substance is that its use be followed by tension reduction and anxiety reduction. Any behavior followed by the easing of stress gets strengthened (negative reinforcement, again). If you add the fact that when you smoke pot you also are apt to get a pleasant feeling of "euphoria," you can really get dependent on the stuff. You can find yourself wanting to be in "La - La Land" all of the time. Both negative reinforcement and positive reinforcement are involved.

Besides, some of your friends will give you all sorts of high fives for showing that you have the courage to challenge your parents, your teachers and even the government on this one. It's fun to show the world that you can do as you please, even if it includes the use of marijuana. Grown-ups use alcohol, don't they? Using pot is no worse. Maybe it ought to be legalized. Maybe the use of marijuana ought to be decriminalized...

It is true that some rather prominent national leaders are calling for the legalization of marijuana and some other psychotropic substances. Notable among them are William

F. Buckley, Jr., the conservative editor of the *National Review* magazine and Milton Freidman, noted conservative professor of economics.

The arguments offered to convince you that legalization is the way to go are sometimes medical, sometimes economic or judicial in nature. Some of the pro-legalization arguments are quite good. They seem to make a lot of good sense, but there are lots of arguments against making the possession and use of marijuana legal that also make good sense. It's difficult for the average teenager to know who is telling the truth.

Which ones are correct? Which ones really make the best sense when you think about what is best for those young people who are inclined to get involved with the use of any mind altering drug? Well, that's for you to decide for yourself...What would you tell your little brother or your sister? Would you want them to experiment with such things? Do you want them to smell like pot smokers? If you don't, then why is it okay for *you?*

Actually, a large number of today's young people have already decided one way or the other, even before they have seriously considered both sides of the issue. Hopefully, you wouldn't do that. Hopefully, you would listen to both sides, then make an intelligent decision.

Is marijuana medically useful in the treatment of any health problems such as glaucoma (a pressure imbalance in the eye)? Can marijuana be used to ease the nausea for terminal cancer patients who must undergo chemotherapy? The answer is yes, possibly, but then other treatments are available that are just as effective if not more so for the treatment of those illnesses. Most doctors would tell you that no medication works the same way for everybody on all occasions.

Would the prescription of marijuana serve as a useful additional option for the physician who must treat these cases? Those who want pot legalized will answer yes to that question. Most physicians, however, will say no. Filling one's lungs with smoke containing nicotine or THC is hardly ever considered as suitable treatment for the seriously afflicted when other options, just as effective, are available for the alleviation of discomfort. Any doctor can find all sorts of other options.

The economic arguments used by those who would decriminalize pot smoking are quite interesting. They are likely to point to the money "wasted" trying to control what they claim is an uncontrollable substance. It is true that billions of dollars have been spent over the years trying to stamp out the marijuana-producing cartels and the pushing of sales to America's youth. The government has not been very successful in its efforts.

As the argument goes, if the profit were taken out of illegal marijuana sales by letting it be commercially produced and taxed as is done with cigarettes and alcohol, the drug lords would stop pushing the stuff. It is a very enticing, but misleading argument. It's not very realistic to assume that those pushers who have become used to living high on drug money would just become law-abiding citizens when profits were no longer available from drug sales. Would they switch to selling drugs that are much worse? Would they give up the drug trade and get honest jobs? Yeah, right... What do *you* think?

"After all," you have often heard it said, "prohibition

didn't work." Is that a good argument in favor of decriminalization? Probably not. What is not admitted to by those in favor of legalization, is the fact that the *repeal* of prohibition didn't work either. The repeal of prohibition didn't solve the alcohol problem. The act of repealing the prohibition of alcohol in the 1930s resulted in a significant *increase* in the production and consumption of alcohol, not a reduction as would be hoped for in the case of the decriminalization of marijuana.

Would a significant increase in the number of pot smokers be good for America? It would seem that if for some weird reason it were desirable to get more and more people to smoke pot, the best way to do it would be to legalize it and make it easy to buy at low cost at any convenience store just like cigarettes and alcohol.

Fifty million Americans smoke legal cigarettes and drink alcohol. Wouldn't it be great if millions upon millions also smoked pot? "It wouldn't happen," say the pot smokers. "It wouldn't happen," said those who wanted repeal of alcohol prohibition in the 30s. "But look what happened in the case of alcohol," say those who do not want to repeat history. They are the ones who don't want to increase the problems society has with pot smokers the way the problems with alcoholism and drunk drivers were increased after the repeal of prohibition.

Would more and more people smoke pot if it were as freely available as cigarettes and alcohol? And would that be a good thing for the young teen-agers of America? Well, that's for you to decide, of course, after you have considered all of the arguments, not before you have taken a little time to think about the consequences.

Drunk drivers kill 18,000 people each year in your country. Would many more die in accidents caused by pot smokers who smoke while driving? You know, any automobile can be considered as a very comfortable mobile smoking lounge, complete with a handy cigarette lighter (not a bottle opener), ash trays and stereo music.

It should be noted that over 40 million people routinely smoke while driving every day. You may feel assured that few of them would drive while smoking euphoria-producing pot cigarettes even if they were available at the convenience market at low cost. You may believe that, but you don't have any way of knowing if it is true.

Most alcohol drinkers say they won't drink and drive. Most pot smokers say they wouldn't smoke pot while driving. Whom should you believe? Would you want your sister to ride home from school in a car driven by a friend who is drinking? How about one who is smoking marijuana? Well, that's for *you* to decide...

Should you smoke that stuff?. Should you take the risk of becoming dependent on pot? Should you support the decriminalization of marijuana?

That's *for you* to decide...

Chapter Four

Mething Up Your Life...

Let's talk about feelings - mostly about feeling good. All of us want to feel good. Teen-agers, especially, want to feel good. They want to feel good about who they are, what they are doing, what the future holds for them and who they will spend it with, but some look for artificial ways to find the "feel good." Some end up seriously hurt.

Some drugs can make you feel good. Temporarily... They are called "uppers." Most young people know that these drugs include the methamphetamines (speed), LSD, cocaine and crack cocaine. They are very powerful drugs that stimulate the user, increasing his activity, hyping him into artificial visions called hallucinations. The high that they produce in the user can be overwhelming to the extent that some people will do weird, aggressive things without being the slightest bit aware of where they are or what they are doing.

Occasionally, a speed user will jump from a tall building like superman. This doesn't occur very frequently, of course, but it is not uncommon for a person under the influence of meth or crack to hurt himself or others without knowing what he is doing. Prisons are filled with many a fellow who intended no harm but ended up by demolishing someone else's property or taking someone's life.

The highs are often followed by prolonged bouts with depression. An effective way to get one's self out of the depression is to take more stimulant drugs. The potential for strong emotional dependence is always there. The user has no sure way of knowing ahead of time if he will be able to maintain control over his use of stimulant drugs.

With frequent use, a speed freak begins to enjoy the highs a bit too much. He is apt to use too much of the drug and risks his life because of increased blood pressure and cardiac-related stress when he is high. Some of the users like the uppers so much that they will die to get them. Some will die because they overdose. In a medical sense, these drugs are very dangerous.

Of course, *you* would not become involved with the use of any of these drugs. You don't want to be a person who is controlled by one of those substances. You are wise enough and mature enough to ignore the claims by your friends that you are "chicken" if you won't try taking LSD just once to see how it feels. You know that for some people, it takes only once to produce a stroke or a heart attack. You can live just fine without your having to prove your courage to your friends by needlessly risking your neck.

Some teen-agers go from one drug to another, always trying to find something that will give them a better kick. Some of them are into designer drugs such as *Ecstacy*. Experimentation with drugs like this is really risky as the user is just taking for granted that whoever did the designing was smart enough to know precisely what he was doing. Sometimes, however, the dosages are wrong and a young life is lost. "This is great stuff," the teen-ager is told by a friend or a pusher who is after money needed to support his own habit. A wise young person just doesn't take the chance.

Cocaine addicts will do anything to get more cocaine. Those into crack cocaine will sell it to their friends and buy it from anyone, even if it means searching it out at crack houses in sleazy neighborhoods filled with unruly gang members who will kill to protect their sources and their supply.

Of all of the dangerous drugs, crack cocaine is the one that is apt to produce the most aggressive, bizarre behavior. Thrown into panic by the unpredictable effects of crack, some addicts will use heroin to "bring them down." That can be a very deadly combination.

Heroin is a really powerful narcotic. Everyone knows that. That means it is a drug that can turn you into an addict totally under its control. When it is injected into the user's bloodstream, heroin causes a "space-out" that is strong enough to hook anyone. Just as happens with nicotine in cigarettes, your blood chemistry will adjust to the presence of heroin in such a way that after awhile your blood is in balance only if heroin is always there.

If you try to get off of heroin, once addicted, you will have to go through the most God-awful heebie-jeebies imaginable. Soon you will know that you were a fool to even think of using the stuff. By then, however, it could be too late.

Would it be better to just try some of it to see how it feels, then to try it again because it feels so good or is it better to take seriously the warnings of others and stay clear of it no matter how good it might feel? Your mom and dad are telling you to stay away from hard drugs and those who use them. Is this one of those mistakes that you want to make for yourself so that you will know what is best for you without having to take the word of your parents? Should your parents just let you learn the hard way?

Should you just go ahead and try it or would it be better to make your decision only after you have carefully thought through the consequences, just in case you are about to make a mistake, big time? Of course, once you are hooked, you might be one of those who could quit taking heroin any time you would want to. You might be the one in a thousand who could get off easily.

Should you try it? Only *you* can decide...

Chapter Five

What About "Safe" Sex ?

Unmarried teen-agers cannot have safe sex. That's right, there's no such thing as safe sex for an unmarried teenager, not if by safe we mean free from any chance of getting pregnant or getting a sexually transmitted disease. There is always risk. Steps can be taken to lower the risk of teen-age pregnancy, but there is always the risk that any teen-age girl having sexual intercourse can become a teen-age mom.

Undoubtedly, you have heard that safe sex is sex that involves the use of protection against making a baby. Undoubtedly, you have been told by some that the use of a condom protects you from having to worry about the possibility of getting pregnant.

Well... Wouldn't it be nice if it were always true? It sure would be great if, so long as you use protection, you could be sure that there was no chance of getting an HIV infection *or* getting pregnant. Wouldn't it be super if the fun and pleasures of having sex had no costly consequences for anyone, especially for *you?*

It just doesn't work that way. There are lots of unwed teen-age mothers around these days. They aren't usually girls who planned to have babies so early in life. Rarely does a young girl say to herself, "I'm gonna have sex with my boyfriend so I can get pregnant." It just happens. Like car accidents just happen to people when they drive without concern for the hazards.

Teenage girls often tend to overlook the real causes of their pregnancies. When asked why they got pregnant, they often reply, "because we didn't use protection." Or they say, "because the condom broke" or "because I forgot to take the pill." Those are not the reasons that pregnancy occurs. Pregnancy does not occur because of what you fail to do. It doesn't happen because you forgot to use a condom or because the condom broke. Pregnancy occurs because of what you *do,* not what you don't do. It occurs because you have sexual intercourse. You don't get pregnant because your protection failed. You get pregnant because you have sex and when you engage in sex, there's always the possibility of pregnancy. It can happen to *any* fertile woman who has sexual intercourse.

Teen-agers often fail to see that when their baby is on the way, it isn't because of what they failed to do, it is because of what they did. They made love by engaging in sexual intercourse when they shouldn't have. They took the risk that it wouldn't happen to them. And it did.

Pointing this out to teen-agers is not meant to be punitive in nature. It really seems as though parents who make this point are sort of kicking the expecting mom when she is already down. It's just a fact of life. If you have sex once, you can get pregnant. If you have sex lots of times, there are lots of chances to get pregnant. If you use protection and have sex, you can *still* get pregnant.

"Everybody's doing it." is the usual claim of those who

are young and are attempting to justify having premarital sex. That, of course, just isn't true. What is true is that some teen-agers are having sex and some are not.

What needs to be asked is if it would be better if more of them did or if more of them did not. That is for you to decide. It is for *you* to decide whether or not you want to take the risk.

No one can deny that sexual expression with someone you love is tremendously stimulating and exciting whether you are sixteen, twenty-six or even in your fifties or sixties. The newness of it when you are just a teen-ager makes it even more so. Who can forget their first love and the wondrous awakening of sexuality that gave them such marvelous feelings? It's difficult to resist the temptations, difficult to say no to one's self and one's partner. It takes great self-discipline to deny *any* of life's great pleasures.

Many young people, even some scholars, choose to dismiss the seriousness of the dilema. They just assume you will go ahead with sex and therefore need counseling in the art of practicing it in a safe manner. "If you're going to do it" says the message, "protect yourself from the possible consequences."

Is it possible that the best way to dependably protect yourself from the consequences is by *not* doing it? Is it possible that the wisest course of action is that which is the least desirable, notably, abstinence? Some laugh at that possibility. However, they may be giving up too easily on the potential for disciplined judgment by most teen-agers of today.

What each teen-ager must ask is if it is wiser to have premarital sex or wiser not to. Of course, that's what any young person in love must decide. It is a most difficult decision. Is this one of those things you should do first, then think about it or think about it first and then decide whether or not to do it? Or, should you just let it happen? Is this one of those decisions where you should let yourself find out from your mistakes what will work and what will not?

What would you tell your sister about all of this? Obviously, she and Jeff are really in love. They're only sixteen, but they are really right for each other. If they asked you to tell them what is best for them (of course, they wouldn't) what would you tell them? Would you tell them to take their chances, just use protection?

You see, everywhere Nancy and Jeff look they see the lure of sex. If they watch a movie, they see beautiful women and handsome men engaging in premarital and adulterous sex without any concern for the consequences. Free-wheeling sex is assumed to be the norm by the most sophisticated T V talk-show hosts and their liberated guests. To be considered "mature," one is to be free of the constraints of society's puritanical authoritarianism. Is it any wonder that Nancy and her boyfriend don't want to miss out on any of the action?

In most discussions about premarital sex, morality, the indicator of right and wrong, tends to be displaced from consideration in favor of a basis for decision-making that is more in accord with what is deemed "socially relevant."

Indeed, it is most rare these days for any talk-show host to express even the slightest concern about the concept of right vs. wrong in a moral sense when discussing the fact that nearly one-third of the babies born in this country today are born to single moms. In many minority communities, fully two-thirds of the babies born have no live-in male role model. With no father to provide guidance for the young male child, that child grows up unguided, often undisciplined and unmanageable.

What does all of this mean *to you?* Does the fact that the movies, the T V talk-shows and even the teachers in school place so little emphasis on the right or wrong of unmarried sexual intimacy mean that you are a fool if you practice abstinence? Should you be ashamed to admit to your friends that you don't (and won't) "do it" when they are pressuring you? Should you feel guilty if your boyfriend demands sex and you are not inclined to give in?

Let's think about this from the boy's perspective and then from that of the girl's. Boys don't usually mean to place their girlfriends at risk in order to gain satisfaction of their own sexual desires. They don't think of it that way. It would be better if they did, but they don't. It isn't as though they plan to get their partners "in a family way."

It's just that the boy's sexual need is so strong, and his partner is so attractive to him that the reasons for abstinence seem too repressive and unrealistic. No one wants to be told what he should not do, least of all the young fellow turned on by all of those raging hormones. A teen-ager overwhelmed by cologne and lace finds it very easy to convince himself and his partner that "protected" sex is safe sex. This, of course, may be true, but, it's too easy to ignore the fact that it may *not* be true...

Not to the credit of boys, they tend to belittle the possible consequences of premarital sex, preferring instead to seek fulfillment with little concern about the dilemma being faced by their partners who must cope with the threat of pregnancy. Remember, that possibility is there for *any* normal woman having sexual intercourse.

It's the girl who frets every month over the real possibility that conception has occurred. It's the young woman, sometimes still almost a child, who will find her world turned upside down if the risk becomes an unfortunate reality. Facing her (and maybe his) parents with unwanted news must be an emotionally traumatic experience for any unwed mother-to-be.

"What do they think of me," she will be asking herself? How could I have been so careless," she will ask, punishing herself, even taking on all of the responsibility in spite of the fact that the boy is equally to blame for prematurely placing both of them in the role of prospective parents.

The burden of raising the child of a teen-age mother frequently goes to the mother's mom. It's not as though Nancy would have planned it that way, it's just that if she must care for the child, she can't regularly attend classes at the high school. She can't work unless there is someone to baby-sit her child. She can't afford the cost of day care. So...Grandma gets to help in the raising of a grandchild she hoped would not be born to her own teenage daughter.

Grandmas love their grandchildren, but they can't help resenting the additional burden placed on their *own* lives at an age when they are beginning to look forward to the easing of their own parental responsibilities. "I've been thinking that my own kids are about raised," they complain, "now I have to raise my daughter's child as well. When do I get *my* freedom?"

"I'll take care of my *own* baby," argues the new mom. Very soon, she learns that she can't do it alone, not if she is intent on finishing her education, not if she plans to get the skills necessary to hold down a well-paying job. Parenthood on the part of a girl too young to handle the responsibility places the young mother at the mercy of those on whom she becomes dependent. Usually the young teen-age mom feels trapped. So does grandma...

If it's Nancy, she will find herself dependent on the government for financial assistance (food stamps and aid for dependent children), on her mother for child care assistance and on her child's father for "family" support that he is often too immature to provide. Nancy herself is trying to meet the demands faced by any adult mom, but she is caught between being a teen-ager and a grown-up.

Because she is not prepared emotionally, educationally or economically by age and experience to care for a child, the young mother, wanting to show that she has become a capable, confident, independent person, finds herself so dependent on help from everyone else that she has little hope of accomplishing her objectives.

While others her age are enjoying the unburdened teen-age life-style, the new mom is hurting from her loss of so much freedom. Confined by the needs of her child, she is suffering from too much responsibility and too much dependency. She is criticized by her own parents who resent her inability to care for her own baby. There is never enough money to buy what she needs for herself and the child without having to plead for help from one source or another. She hates having to beg all of the time.

Nancy's boyfriend may not be around much anymore. Being a young dad was not in the cards for Jeff. Besides, he has a new girlfriend now.

Jeff isn't really a monster in all of this. It's just that he, too, soon realizes that he is too young and too inexperienced to handle the financial and emotional needs of a family. He says he loves his child, but he still tends to distance himself, then eventually walks away. Jeff can do that; Nancy cannot. He can be sorry, but absent. Nancy must carry on, struggling to regain some sense of respect for herself.

It's customary today to use this kind of unfortunate dilemma as justification for a decision that would free the young woman once again to resume being a carefree high school student, free of the stresses of parenthood. You have already anticipated the idea of having an abortion, terminating the pregnancy in the early stage so as to give the pregnant teen-ager a new beginning, a chance to get on with life, wiser and more mature than before.

Some would say abortion is an appropriate way to deal with the stresses of an unwanted pregnancy. Others say it becomes an emotionally injurious memory with lasting effects. Imagine yourself having to make that kind of decision... What would *you* decide? What would you tell Nancy to decide?

Of course, none of this would ever happen to Nancy, nor to *you*. Hopefully, you are a young person who knows that in some ways having premarital sex is like taking drugs. There are all sorts of temptations out there that can get you into a whole heap of trouble.

The drug-induced "highs" can become depressing lows. The sexual orgasms can become a pregnancy. Freedoms carelessly expressed can become the seed for dependency on others.

What a dilemma for a teen-ager! Have you ever asked yourself why life has to be so damned complicated? Well... It just *is*. There's not very much you can do to simplify it.

There is, however, much you can do to make it even more complex, making yourself more and more miserable.

You can increase your risk of chemical dependency by smoking cigarettes, smoking pot and experimenting with uppers and downers. You can add to your life the risk of unwanted pregnancy by engaging in premarital sex that you know is unwise and that you should be considering as wrong. You can ignore the dangers and just let life happen...

Then happen, it will. It will happen to countless numbers of young people who will make decisions that fail to reflect a willingness to say "No" to themselves and to their friends. What will it be for *you?* Only you can decide if a stable, productive, self-sufficient future is worth what it costs. You must decide if you are willing to discipline yourself *now* for a better life as an adult.

Self-denial is not fun. Self-control is not acquired automatically. Those who have it, earned it. Those who do not, didn't. Self-control doesn't make you happy for the short term. It doesn't give you what you want *now.*

Self-control and self-discipline are what protect you from yourself. They protect your future. They are what distinguish the child from the adult. They imply a willingness to put off instant gratification as demanded by the child in favor of the setting and the fulfilling of long-term goals, as is done by the mature adult.

Self-control and self-discipline require respect for authority rather than resistance to it. If you are a mature citizen you recognize that there are some things that are okay to do because they are right, but some things that you should *not* do because you know that they are wrong. Learning which is which and conducting yourself accordingly is the way you keep unnecessary complications out of your life.

Chapter Six

Sexual Abstinence or Condomination

To Jake, it seems as though Melissa is dedicating herself to driving him out of his cotton pickin' mind. If only she didn't pour herself into those incredibly bad looking jeans! Man, how he gets turned on when he sees her in those hot lookin' jeans! She's really something, don't you know, like, what's a guy to think? What's a guy to do?

Melissa is perplexed because Jake always wants to get too close, wanting to do a little more than just huggin' and kissin'. But oh, when Jake gets to doing more than just huggin' and kissin', it's really like, "Wow!" that's really somethin' else! What's a girl to think? What's a girl to do?

Everybody says, "Just go for it," but if you go for it, sometimes you get it. Then you're in a heap of trouble. There's that dilemma, again...

On TV, they just sleep around with everyone, just about any time and anywhere. It's all so romantic and so delicious. No problem, just don't get caught! In real life, it's also romantic and delicious, but by the millions teenagers are getting caught. They are finding themselves in a family way, are getting genital herpes or are contracting serious sexually transmitted diseases.

Why does Melissa have to be so pretty and why is she so

tempting all of the time? Why does Jake have to be so turned on to her all of the time? "God, she's a doll," he says. "Just can't leave that girl alone." "He's a real hunk," she gushes. "Nobody should have a body like hers," he says. "His boyish grin just takes me apart," she sighs. Is it any wonder there's trouble in River City? What's a couple to do?

Cold showers (alone), picnics (chaperoned) and goofy golf won't cut it. It's going to take more than those things to keep the hormones under control. But then, who *wants* to keep the hormones under control? Not teen-agers Jake or Melissa. They're too much in love. What they want is to enjoy their relationship to the max...

So kissin' and huggin' becomes intimate petting and intimate petting becomes intercourse. That's the way it is in River City. And everywhere else, for that matter... It would be great if that's all there were to it. Wouldn't it be super if all of those good things didn't end up as bad things? It would be great if the fun things couldn't have any painful consequences.

Time to get real, isn't it? Lots and lots of teen-agers are pushing their own kid-filled strollers around the malls these days. Lots of kids in love are finding themselves saddled with responsibilities that they didn't expect and that they are too young to handle. Lots of them are losing their self-esteem because they have to keep asking mom and dad to take care of *their* babies. Lots of teen-agers are begging for diaper money because they can't work, go to school and be parents at the same time. Lots of them are simply trapped as a result of their inability to say "no" to themselves. Could it happen to *you*?

Parents often harp on the ever-present dangers faced by

their teen-agers. Teen-agers are quick to tell the parents not to worry. "No big deal, mom," they say. "We'll be careful…" Parents know that their sons and daughters can easily get lost in the excitement of their intimate relationships. Mom and dad are in a quandary over how to steer their kids into adulthood free from regrets, free from too much responsibility too soon. They like to think that their teen-agers will become adults first, then parents later, when they are more mature and more capable. It does work better for everyone that way.

Melissa's parents would like to give her a nice wedding when she is a bit more mature, would like to see her with a loving live-in husband and would like to be the grandparents of a few well-adjusted kids, kids who go home with their mom *and* their dad at the end of any visit.

Single moms *can* raise good kids. It's just that they are much less apt to be able to do so if they are unmarried and have no steady income and no regular dad for the kids to relate to. Four out of 10 children in America presently have no dad to kiss them goodnight! There's no dad to tell their troubles to, no dad to reassure them that they are good kids. Is it any wonder that so many young boys seek male guidance by becoming members of gangs?

Parents, teachers and community leaders would like to adopt policies that would help teen-agers avoid adding unnecessary complications to their lives, but wonder how they can get through to their kids. What should they be saying to their teen-agers about premarital sex?

If they want to see fewer teen-agers becoming unwed mothers and want to see more children raised in families with dependable incomes and want to see all kids raised by parents who stress good moral values, they may have to get a better understanding of their *own* objectives.

What should be the goal for all parents who want to keep their teen-agers out of the trouble that comes from undisciplined sex? What should be their main objective? Should they work to increase the number of teen-agers who practice "safe" sex even though they know that no protection is foolproof, that even the condom is often ineffective in preventing pregnancy and disease?

If so, then the best approach would be to give out condoms at schools and to assure the teen-agers that sex is okay (or, at least more so) if only they use "protection." Perhaps, they should say that premarital sex is *not* okay, but is safer if they use "protection."

Or, should the objective be different? Perhaps the objective should be to get fewer(not more) fourteen and fifteen year-olds to engage in sexual intercourse, "protected" or otherwise.

If that is the better objective, then, the *worst* thing that parents, teachers and counselors could do is convince the teen-agers that premarital sex is "safe" and provide them with the means to have sex while convincing themselves that the dangers are thereby significantly reduced.

In the past, the major influences that have discouraged teen-agers from giving in to the powerful temptation to have sex included the fear of pregnancy, likely social disgrace and the threat of catching a sexually transmitted disease. We might wonder if, as the fear of what can happen with undisciplined sex is reduced by the promise of safety, the temptation to give in to one's personal sexual desires is increased? As the fear of pregnancy is reduced, is its strong disciplining influence also reduced?

Is it a wise thing to convince fourteen and fifteen year-olds that pregnancy, social disgrace and disease are less likely to occur as a result of sexual intercourse today (especially with "protection") when the actual rate of unwed pregnancy today is over four times what it was just twenty years ago? Over one million teen-agers get pregnant each year in America. Over 400,000 of those are terminated by abortion. Are teen-agers finding premarital sex to be safer these days?

Let's dig a bit deeper into the logic of those who feel earnestly that teen-agers should be encouraged to practice safe sex (if they are going to have sex). It is entirely possible that their well-intended recommendation represents a major mistake in public policy. Many more teen-agers are engaging in sexual intercourse today, for a variety of reasons. One of those reasons, likely, is the assurance that it can be made safe when it can only be made safer.

"Protection" does not eliminate the chance of pregnancy, at best it only reduces the odds of it happening. Therefore, the false sense of security it gives may be breaking down the barriers to undisciplined sexual activity that, in earlier generations, resulted in fewer unwed moms and in fewer fatherless children.

Teen-age premarital sexual intercourse involves gambling with the prospect of pregnancy and disease. "Protection" is just a gamble with better odds. Do you know what happens to those who gamble? They tend to get hooked on gambling. They gamble more and more and eventually many more lose.

Knowing this, should parents, teachers and counselors be providing teen-agers with *any* means for reducing the influences that do help them to discipline their sexual behavior? Perhaps the selling of "protection" and the assurance of "safer" sex has been a major mistake of the 80s and 90s that has contributed significantly to the increase in unwanted pregnancies and disease in America. Should fourteen and fifteen year-olds be gambling *at all?* Should parents and others be telling them to "be protected?" If so, surely, the best protection is to *not* gamble at all... *That's* the most important message of all.

How do you feel about this? What do *you* think the objectives of parents, teachers and sex counselors should be? What would *you* recommend?

It's a tough call, isn't it? Yet, if one-third of all babies born today are born into fatherless homes and two-thirds of all minority babies are born to unwed mothers and the occurrence of unwed teen-age pregnancies is reaching astounding rates at all socioeconomic levels everywhere in America, it is a call that *must* be made.

What would *you* recommend?

Would you recommend encouraging more young people to use protection for safer sex? Or, would you recommend programs that stress abstinence and personal self-discipline as the best way to avoid the pitfalls?

Which is the best way to affect a change in a positive direction for America's teen-agers? Which one would *you* choose? If you were trying to be a responsible parent for your own sixteen year-old son and your fourteen year-old daughter, what would you recommend for *them?*

Chapter Seven

Question Authority? Yeah! Right...

"Why not just make drugs legal? Why do we need laws that make criminals out of people who just want to do their things? And, while we're at it, why do we have to have laws that force us to wear a helmet when we ride our Harleys? And, oh yeah, why do we have to wear our seat belts even if we don't want to? And, why should anyone else be telling us how to live our sex-lives? It's nobody else's business.

After all, it's *my* head that gets busted if I'm stupid enough to overdose on meth or if I crunch my hog into a tree. It's like the government has to control everything I do, so that there isn't any freedom anymore."

Does that sound familiar? Do some of your friends sound like that? Have you heard kids say that they only hurt *themselves* when they put themselves at risk? It just isn't true. Anyone with any brains whatever knows that it isn't true. If anyone gets seriously injured or actually dies, a lot of people get hurt. Parents hurt terribly. Brothers and sisters hurt. Friends hurt.

If you attend the funeral of a young person who lost his life because he would not follow reasonable rules of conduct you will see the faces of people who are overwhelmed with grief. Surely, they are not just hurt. They are angry as well. They are mad because their son, brother or friend showed so little consideration for *them* and he was so wrapped up in his own macho selfishness that he thought he was invincible, but he wasn't.

He drove recklessly to show off how much courage he thought he had. Or, he had to carry a gun in his car. He experimented with drugs and lost control. Now he's dead. Perhaps he drank so much that he actually destroyed his liver and immune system. And now he's dead. He couldn't be bothered with rules that might have saved his life. He couldn't be considerate enough to play it safe so as to avoid causing great pain for other people, the people who cared about *him*.

Disregard for danger is often seen by the teen-ager as a sign of courage, a behavior pattern that gets respect from peers. A teen-ager is apt to be applauded if he can guzzle more beers than his buddies, if he can be quicker and more effective at throwing karate chops than his adversaries or if he can boast about his great numbers of girlfriends. On the movie screen and on TV, the macho male martial arts expert with lots of female "trophies" is shown as an adventurous hero.

Wouldn't it be better if, instead, teen-agers gave each other "high fives" when they showed consideration for those who *do* care about them ? Teen-agers should earn the respect of their peers by doing things that are right, not the things that are risky or wrong. They could earn some respect by trying to avoid the taking of unnecessary risks. They could do this by *not* violating reasonable rules and by *not* challenging authority at every opportunity. They could treat each other with respect.

Boys should not be respected for the number of girls they have disrespected. They should be respected for the self-discipline they have shown in their relationships with girls. Girls should *demand* respect from those teenage boys they date and tell them in no uncertain terms that they will have nothing to do with boys who abuse or take advantage of them in any way.

It would be nice if young people could grow up in a world that did not have so many temptations. However, it would surely be a dull world. Few would want a world where boys and girls felt no sexual attraction to each other. Yet, most know that uncontrolled sexual attraction can result in frightening problems for teen-agers not seriously considering the consequences of their behavior.

Boys need to be made aware that they do not express love for their girlfriends by placing on them unreasonable demands for sex. They cannot have easy, immediate gratification of their sexual needs without risking the stability and sometimes the security of their partners.

Unmarried teen-age girls need to be made aware that they have a right (and a responsibility) to say "No," and that it is the wise thing to do. They need to know that boys who will not take "No" for an answer are best avoided. Unmarried teen-age girls need to be reassured that just *not* doing it is much wiser than just giving in to a boy's demands.

Sounds "old fashioned," doesn't it? Like old fashioned values, and all that... Maybe those who promote for sexual abstinence for the unmarried teen-ager rather than "safe" sex just don't know how it is today, what with all of the sex on T V, with condoms and pills for "protection" and a new kind of morality that is not so restrictive.

Well, maybe... Or, maybe those who support abstinence know something that some others also know, but do not choose to emphasize. It is the lesson, ages old but forever true, that self-discipline and self-denial in accordance with reasonable rules is a social positive, not a social negative.

They know that the children in a society are more secure emotionally if the distinction between what is right and what is wrong is not obscured by attempts to make rights out of wrongs. They know and accept that some things are just wrong and that it is not appropriate to believe everyone who tries to show you that wrongs are "relative," okay sometimes, not okay at other times, depending on what if... Okay, if you just use "protection."

In today's entertainment-oriented society, teen-agers constantly see immediate self-gratification portrayed as the routine, usually accepted life-style. Premarital and extramarital sex, once viewed as wrong, are now seen as justifiable simply because it is undesirable to deny the need for personal expression. Control over one's own desires, whether by others or by one's self, is viewed as oppressive and unrealistic.

Let's look at how it works. Have you ever noticed how easy it is to say "Yes" to yourself and how much you don't want to accept the word "No?" It sure is easy to buy what you can't afford, to go where you want to go, but shouldn't, to do what you want to do even though you have been advised by others that it's not too swift a move for you.

That's because wants are powerful things. Certainly, it's real easy to convince yourself that what you want is what you need. It's easier for you to be influenced in the direction of what you want than to deny yourself what you shouldn't have. It's hard to accept limitations on the good things, just awful to miss out on any of the fun and the excitement of living.

So, when temptations arise, as they often do, you find it convenient to ease up on the rules as they apply to yourself, even though those rules may make good sense as you would want them applied to others. It's almost always possible to find a few positive reasons why you should do what you want to do. It's very easy to simply avoid consideration of the reasons why you should *not* do what you want to do.

Those who see right vs. wrong as relative, i.e., always depending on the *"if"* of things, make it easy for young people to justify what they are doing that is wrong by convincing themselves that what is wrong is not really as much so, in view of the changing times. They stress what they want. They sell "enlightened" attitudes of those who wish to free us from constraints recommended by "old fashioned" parents and teachers. What used to be considered as wrong way back then is not as much so today, especially if you consider what others do all of the time.

The result of this process, as viewed over, say, the last fifty years has been a significant lowering of standards in society and a decrease in the number of people who accept and respect appropriate values. "After all," as the argument goes, "it's 2012, not the 50s. Things have changed. What was forbidden in the 50s is not considered as seriously wrong today." People are less constrained, more open, more expressive and less guilt-ridden today. People do things today without much concern about what other people think.

Few would deny the truth of this. What is not certain, however, is if the easing of constraints (the acceptance of more permissive attitudes by young people) has been as good for the teen-agers of today as the liberators would have everyone believe.

It is nice to be less guilt-ridden today. It's nice to be able to do things today that your parents wouldn't have let themselves do for fear that the parish priest, their parents or the school principal would bring down the awful wrath of God upon them. In the "old" days, they would have to suffer from the scorn of their peers who would point to them accusingly if they didn't respect the social conventions. Lord, help you, if you got caught being too familiar with Freddie while mom and dad were at church!

Some view this long, much overdue progression away from the stodgy old rules of the ancients (parents) as good for society as a whole. Less restriction means more comfort. More freedom means more creativity. More liberation means more sophistication. To be "in" is to be uninhibited and expressive. To be "out" is to be reserved, cautious and controlled. It's more fun to be free, less fun to be regulated.

Who is to decide which is better? What will *you* decide? It isn't difficult to figure out what the average person *wants*. The wants tend toward freedom, the freedom to do as we please. It's easy to see those wants as needs, the need to be unregulated by anyone, by the government, by a set of well-meaning parents, by teachers or even by our concerned friends. Perhaps, we are even reluctant to regulate ourselves!

Arguments are easily constructed in support of being free, because freedom is more closely aligned with what we want. It's much more difficult to build a strong set of values that requires a willingness to respect rules that limit our own self-interests, let alone to show a determination to discipline ourselves in the interest of concern for others.

Take the teen-ager's "need" for premarital sex, for example. Perhaps no other topic more clearly illustrates the desire young people have to build arguments in favor of what they want, even at the expense of what is right.

Think of the argument that sex can be made safe by using a condom. Few teen-agers would wish for that argument *not* to be true. Therefore, they are inclined to believe it and to behave accordingly.

The message sent by those who are more liberal on the subject is "If you are going to have sex, you should use a condom." That, however, is not the message received by the young person who wants to have premarital sex. The message received, instead, is the one that he wants to hear. The received message is, "It is safer and less harmful and, therefore, *less wrong* to have sex if you use a condom." It is implied that smart teen-agers use a condom, whereas, those less smart don't protect themselves or their partners at all.

Teen-agers want to hear this message. It gives them the

freedom to do what they want. What they don't want to hear is what is *really* true. The safest and smartest teen-agers are those who make the decision not to have premarital sex without or *with* a condom.

Again, does this sound old-fashioned? What do *you* think? What is better for your society as a whole? Are teen-agers better off when the rules are less restrictive? Any fairly objective consideration of this problem requires that we decide if young people are happier and more stable today than they were in the 50s. Are today's teen-agers really better off now than they were then?

What do *you* think? Is society better off if teen-age pregnancy, which results in a significant loss of freedom for the teen-age girl, has become so common that nearly one-third of all babies born are born to single moms? If two-thirds of the babies born in minority communities have no live-in father, is society better off?

Will problems with juvenile crime, drug abuse and alcohol addiction go down by the year 2050 if, by that time, half of the children in America are being raised in fatherless homes? Are fathers necessary or is it perfectly okay if mom runs the show? What do *you* think?

Is it better if there are fewer families in America with an adult male present to serve as a role model, especially for those young boys in need of appropriate guidance? What do *you* think? Do you think that it is better if more and more young people are more and more free to experiment with drugs? Is it better if teen-agers don't feel any repressive guilt if they smoke pot, drink alcohol, sleep with their friends and dedicate themselves to keeping their parents in a panic?

Wouldn't it be great if teen-agers could avoid all of those socially undesirable behaviors without the need for any repressive parental influence? Wouldn't it be great if just on their own advice they didn't pay the tobacco executives for getting them addicted to nicotine? Wouldn't it be super if, on their own, they decided to refrain from premarital sex, just because it is wrong? It sure would be great if they did only the smart things, just out of consideration for their parents and just for the sake of being good kids.

Well now... That isn't very realistic, is it? That's just not gonna happen, right? That's like a happy heart attack. Get real, again...

So what do *you* recommend? Now, don't just say, "I dunno," That's what teen-agers usually answer. *You can* do better than that. Think up a good way to keep teen-agers on the right track, preferably a way that involves teaching them that some things are surely wrong for them to do and that they *should* be disappointed in themselves if they do them. We don't want them feeling guilty now, do we? Or, *do* we? What do *you* think about this?

Think up a way to keep teen-agers from doing all of those risky things that they do while they convince themselves that wrong things are right if they just say that "everyone else is doing them."

Why does society need rules that limit you from doing all of the things that you want to do? And why do we need to punish those who break those rules? Because, if everyone makes his or her own rules or if an individual refuses to follow reasonable rules, others (parents, friends and even strangers) pay for the undisciplined person's disorder. No one lives as an island unto himself. What *you* do affects others.

Ignoring reasonable rules of conduct, an undisciplined drinker can kill someone who is innocent. A selfish, drug-oriented teen-ager can victimize his parents and others. A boy demanding sex with his girlfriend can endanger her self-respect and threaten her with the possibility of an unwanted pregnancy. It would seem that, as the rules are eased and society accepts behavior that is less and less respectful of others, there are prices that must be paid. The undisciplined expressions of some infringe on the security of others. Respect for rules and for authority, if expected (and even demanded) by society, tends to moderate the cost of indiscretion.

None of these things mentioned would happen to *you,* of course, but they could happen to your brothers, sisters or to your friends. Wouldn't those you love be less likely to get themselves into serious trouble if they recognized the importance of rules and the wisdom of respect for authority? What do *you* think?

You know, one of the truly nice things about young people today is the fact that most actually *will* follow reasonable rules, if the rules make sense and are fairly enforced. In fact, most teen-agers really want clearly defined guidelines for what is right and what is wrong. Most teenagers abide by those rules.

So, what about *you? Are* you one of those who respects authority or are you fighting it at every opportunity? Do you see the value of having rules that are enforceable or do you feel that everyone should be free to do as he or she pleases regardless of how it affects others?

How do *you* feel about this?

Chapter Eight

Havin' a Attitude...

Some kids get an attitude. It gets in the way of everything they try to do. They get angry and carry resentment wherever they go. They feel cheated and act as if the whole world is trying to get the best of them. They get aggressive, thinking that the only way to get along is to fight. They waste most of their creative energy by resisting all authority. They listen only to those who try to make themselves appear special by turning away from the ways of the establishment.

Are you one of those who feels resentful? Are you one who is always mad because nothing is going your way? Life really sucks, doesn't it? Maybe *you* got a attitude... Maybe you should think about whether or not you *want* to live out your days with an attitude...

One day, a psychology teacher (that's right, the author of your little book) was teaching a morning class to a few sleepy students who were interested in being anywhere else except in class. It was a beautiful day, the kind of day when young boys should be out playing volleyball or chasing young girls around the mall. A great day for being at the park, tossing frisbees, anything but sitting in a stuffy classroom trying not to listen to an old psychology professor who had long since forgotten what it's like to be young.

The professor was talking about *attitude*. "Attitude," he said, "can be either positive or negative." You can choose how you want it to be for *yourself*. You can make your own mental outlook be negative and sad by constantly pointing to all of the bad things in the world and by trying to show others how unfair life is. Especially to *you*... After awhile, it will become automatic for you.

Everything you look at will appear negative. Why? Well, because that's what you are looking for, so, that's what you will find.

"Or," said the professor, "you can choose to take note of the many good things that exist in your life," like parents who care about you, like football games, the Burger King and french fries, like the fact that you live in a country where there's lots of opportunity to get ahead if you work to achieve. You can look forward to getting a driver's license and owning a car. You can have a telephone and fall in love. You can even get a credit card.

If you keep looking at the positive things around you, you are apt to see more and more of them. Why? Well, because that's what you are looking for... You will be a person who chooses to look at life in a positive way and you will be a person who is more likely to find what you are looking for. You will be more apt to find the good things in life.

You see, the kind of attitude you develop about life is a kind of self-fulfilling prophecy (as the psychologists often call it). You can make it good or bad, however you choose. If you want to be a negative person, just keep pointing to all of the negative things in the world. You will find what you are looking for because, let's face it, there are lots of sad things to think about and you'll be looking for them. You will spend lots of time on the self-pity pot...

Wouldn't it be a good idea for you to think a little more positively about your life? Wouldn't it be a good idea to make a conscious decision about whether you want to be a positive or negative person? You are most likely to find the things *that you are looking for.* It's up to you to decide what's best for you.

Oh, but what about that psychology professor? Well, suddenly that morning, the strangest thing happened as the professor went on and on with his dull lecture about the importance of thinking positively about life. Everyone in the class was startled by the noisy crashing sound of a large bird hitting the window near the front of the room. As everyone looked on, the bird crashed again into the outside of the window pane as the glass abruptly interfered with its flight. Ouch? That must have hurt!

A little moth was fluttering against the inside of the glass, apparently trying to get outside to escape from the professor's lecture. The glass prevented that hungry bird from enjoying a delicious moth-a-meal.

When the bird crashed against the glass yet a third time, a bored male student in the back of the room exclaimed, "What a dumb, stupid bird." A young lady who was sitting in the front row interpreted the situation in a very different way. "Wow," she yelled, "What a lucky moth!"

Isn't it interesting how each student witnessing the same situation saw it so differently? Why would that be so? Why would one person automatically tend to see that scenario so negatively while another was inclined to see it so positively? How would *you* have seen it? Why do some people see life in a negative way, while others see it with more good than bad? Some people work at living a happy, positive life. Others seem to let themselves fall into sadness and despair. Some people never learn that happiness is something you must earn, something you must work to attain. They spend their lives waiting for it to come to them and they are disappointed when it doesn't. What a disappointment it must be, to wait for it year after year and see it in others, but not in yourself...

Which way will it be for *you?* Which way do you *want* it to be?

You, too, can have an *attitude.* One that's positive or one that's negative. It can work for you or it can work against you. Which way would be better for *you?* How do you *want* it to be? Are you willing to work to get it that way?

When do you think you should begin?

Here's what it's all about. It's about whether you want to be in control of your life or whether you want to let a variety of chemicals like nicotine, alcohol, THC, cocaine or heroin control *you.*

It's tempting to show your friends and your parents how grown up and free you can be by freely using cigarettes, alcohol, pot, meth and whatever else, but then you could lose your freedom by getting hooked. Some of your friends are already hooked.

It has to do with whether you want to live your own life free from dependence on dope or if you are willing to live as a slave to cigarettes, alcohol and drugs that can destroy you.

It has to do with whether you want to continue to be free to make your own good decisions or if you would rather just spend your life paying for your bad ones.

There is so much that you can do with your life if you remain in control of as much of it as is possible. If you search for artificial thrills and cheap "kicks" through the use of psychotropic substances that offer easy escape from life's challenges, you will be copping out at the same time that others are facing life head on. You will be learning how to hide, rather than how to live. Others, wiser than you, will be leaving you behind.

It has to do with independence. People who get hooked on alcohol, cocaine, amphetamines, etc., can't live independent lives. Over and over again, others have to rescue them from themselves. Alcohol and drug oriented people have trouble keeping their jobs, paying their bills and meeting their responsibilities. They become a chronic pain to other members of their families and to their friends. They become dependent on others to keep them out of trouble. It seems as though they are not able to mature enough to become independent or self-sufficient. *You* could be like that... Just live your life undisciplined.

Of course, there are cigarettes, beer, bourbon and vodka available at any convenience store. Marijuana is obtainable everywhere. Cocaine and meth are easy to find if you just ask around. Across from the school yard you can get *Ecstacy*.

You can go for them with gusto. You can "just do it." Or you can think these things through, then decide that you want to stay clear.

Again, only *you* can decide what is right for you.

Is your relationship with your parents a good one? Do

they seem to respect you and do you respect them or is there an atmosphere of resentment present that seems to get in the way of any real supportive communication between the generations? Are mom and dad so busy making a living that they don't help you with your problems? Are they interested at all in your problems? Are you interested in *theirs?*

Do you ever think of *their* problems? Teen-agers are not inclined to do that, you know...Teen-agers don't usually feel responsible for what their parents do. It's not that they don't care, it's just that parents are just assumed to be capable of doing everything right.

You do love them. So let's assume that you do hate to see them make any major mistakes that might affect them or affect *your* family. If your mom and dad got themselves into trouble, would you try to help them? After all, they *are* your parents. If you saw your mom about to do something she shouldn't, would you tell her to watch out? Would you warn her of the dangers? If your dad was drinking too much and it was affecting the stability of your dad and mom's marriage would you just look the other way? Or would you feel a responsibility to tell your dad to shape up? Of course, he might not listen, but would you be willing to try?

Let's assume that you would try to help mom or dad make good decisions simply because you love them and want them to remain safe and happy. That's what most young people would do for their parents. Would you do that for *your* parents?

If that's what you would do, then why shouldn't your parents try to warn you when you are about to screw up your life by getting too involved with cigarettes, alcohol or drugs? Is it unreasonable for them to love you and want to see you remain safe and happy? Or do you think that when they see you heading for the pits they too should just look the other way? Certainly, they have lots of other things to think about, don't they?

What kind of parents do you want? Do you want a mom and dad who don't give a damn what you do, or parents who love you enough to tell you that some of the things you are doing are out of line? Do you want parents who ignore you or do you want your parents to teach you what is right? Do you want some one to love you enough to show you how to get a good life?

Think about these things before you put up a wall between yourself and the parents who love you so much. They want to express their love by offering you the benefit of their experience. Think about whether or not you are going to let them down.

Grown-ups do know more about what is important in life simply because they have been around longer and have seen more of the troubles that people get themselves into when they fail at life management.

There are exceptions, of course. Some parents are not very good at parenting. It's a tough job, tougher than any young person can know. Your mom and dad, however, are probably pretty good people who want you to get a life, not buy a death. They know that young teen-agers who look for artificial ways to get thrills often do so because they don't have the courage to live life drug free.

Parents know that life is better lived by those who opt for good discipline rather than free-wheeling good times Should you let yourself get hooked on cigarettes, alcohol or drugs or should you spend time thinking about the implications of these things before you start, then make the decision to keep your freedom?

Only *you* can decide...

The person who smokes two packs of cigarettes a day is not a free person. He (or she) is controlled by the habit. The alcoholic is not a free person. He becomes a slave to his need for his beer, vodka or whatever.

An older person may no longer have a choice as to how his life will be with regard to cigarettes and alcohol. As a younger person, *you* may still have some say so as to how your life will be lived. Will you decide your fate wisely and stay substance free or will you just go along with the friends who do what is not so bright?

Will you be more influenced by your smoking and drinking friends who get kicks by challenging the system or by your parents who know that learning to play by the rules of the system leads to a more fulfilling and rewarding life, one free from dependencies?

Maybe you are one who will "just do it," but then, maybe you aren't. Maybe you are one who will think a bit first, before it's too late. Maybe you are one who is mature enough to play it cool...

It's up to you. Only *you* can decide what kind of life is best for you.

Chapter Nine

About Feeling Depressed

Sometimes, life really sucks. That's right, it seems like it's hardly worth the effort. There are so many pressures, so many problems, so many people trying to tell you what to do and what to think that it's nearly impossible to keep your head on straight. Everyone wants you to do things their way, no one lets you think for yourself.

Have you ever felt that way? Well, join the club. Have you ever felt overwhelmed by all of the demands placed on you and do you feel that no one wants to give you credit for anything you accomplish? Why keep going on when no one notices what you do? Why continue to tolerate the criticism and the bullying of other people when it just makes you hurt?

During the teen-age years most kids get quite depressed from time to time. It sort of comes with the territory, as they say, and it doesn't feel good at all. Some get so depressed that they give up and actually take their own lives. Some are so threatened by the fear of being criticized and even laughed at by others their own age that they decide that life is just not worth living. Some teen-agers even think about killing themselves. That's so sad, so wasteful of human life and it can result in tragic effects on the suicide's family and their well-meaning friends.

The national statistics of teen-age suicide tell the extent of the tragedy across America. Over 30,000 kids take their own lives each year. They do it for a wide variety of reasons, some related to conflicts within their own families, many over their difficulties at school. They may feel excluded from the approval of other students. They want to fit in, but for some reason they cannot. Some experience embarrassing criticsim from bullies who roam the internet to find ways to make others miserable. Vicious, nasty comments about anyone presented on Facebook can have a devastating effect on the self image of a teen-ager who needs support as he or she interacts with peers at school or within their own neighborhoods.

Bullying may be great fun for the bully, but it can lead to tragedy within a family when a victim becomes overwhelmed by mean-spirited ridicule. All teens should be made to clearly understand that they have a responsibility to be sensitive to the feelings of others, even those they don't like.Taking advantage of anyone by sending painful messages about them on Facebook is a cruel thing to do. Those who choose to do so should be punished.

But, what should *you* do as a young person who finds the dark feelings of depression coming over you, hurting you and making you feel inadequate and unappreciated? Should you just turn inward on yourself, letting the negative feelings of limited self-worth erode your confidence about who you are and what you can do with your life? Of course not!

Maybe, just maybe, a tired old college professor

psychologist can make a few suggestions that might be helpful.

Now, don't get your hopes up too much, because there are no real guarantees that these suggestions will work to ease the pain. But, they just might, so what have you got to lose by listening to them?

First of all, lets consider the fact that as a teen-ager, you are physically preparing yourself for the role of a prospective adult and parent and that your body is adjusting to that future role and responsibility. There are a number of changes in your blood chemistry that begin to occur in the teens that will affect your moods and even your attitude about life. Sometimes you will feel sad and depressed and you might not even know why.

You didn't have to worry about those feelings as much when you were just a grade-school child, but its different now as you become a grown up person. The changes in your blood are called hormonal changes and they will make you moody and irritable from time to time, but those feelings will come and go. They are quite normal. Not to worry.

So when you are experiencing those down feelings, you should be assured that the feelings will only be with you for awhile. Some teens think that if they get depressed, they are abnormal. That's not necessarily true. You are not alone. All normal teen-agers have that problem to some extent.

Even if you are a little bit different, don't let anyone convince you that you are a nerd. You are not! You are just as good as anyone else and you are entitled to be treated fairly and with respect. All teen-agers are valuable. All teen-agers have great potential. All teen-agers should be encouraged to feel good about themselves.

If you are being bullied by someone at school, don't be afraid to talk to your favorite teacher or school counselor about it. Tell your parents how you feel. They can put pressure on those who are mean to you and make them stop.

As you get a little bit older, that is, into young adulthood you will get a better understanding of yourself. You will gain more confidence and be less concerned about dumb criticism by others. You will become capable of standing up for yourself.

It takes time. It's all part of growing up.

Chapter Ten

Academic Entrapment

Do you feel that you are trapped in school? If so, you're not alone. In the late high school years, some teen-agers want to quit school altogether, get a job and start living on their own. They are impatient and want to get on with their lives. This means escaping from dull, demanding teachers who insist that they learn dumb things that seem to have no connection at all with the real world, the world of work, freedom and independence.

"Jobs are everywhere," some say, "and I can do all sorts of things to take care of myself. It's better than sitting in the classroom all day doing nothing."

Billy is one of those restless teen-agers. He can't see why he should be required to learn things like history when he can't change it, math that a calculator or computer can do for him or geography and literature that bore him silly. After all, he can get a job *now* bustin' tires, tossing burgers or digging trenches for the local cable company. Lots of service stations need car repair help.

"If I work full time," he argues, "I can get my own apartment, have my own car and I won't have to lean on mom and dad anymore." Bill feels that if he's on his own, he can make his own decisions and he won't have to listen endlessly to all of those who are telling him how he should be living his life.

Actually, Bill is quite sharp. He handles himself quite well for someone who is only sixteen. He figures that if he needs smarts from professionals, he will just hire them as needed. Meanwhile, he will be one who is actually *doing* something rather than just studying about things at school.

Bill isn't entirely wrong in his thinking. He *can* do a lot of things just the way he is. He can be a good, productive employee. He can earn a living and pay his bills. It's going to be a lot harder for him to do so, however, if he doesn't finish high school.

It used to be that a high school diploma was the ticket to a fair entry level job that got you started toward a challenging career. It isn't that way anymore. It sure would be nice if it were, but it isn't. You are at a disadvantage now if you don't have a diploma plus at least a two-year community college degree, just to keep up.

United States Census Bureau statistics illustrate at the present time that most professionals who have advanced degrees get paid salaries that are as much as ten times those of the average high school dropout. On an average basis, those completing a two-year Associate in Arts Degree following high school earn approximately twice as much as those who do not bother to get a high school diploma. Clearly, many advantages in life go to those who prepare well for a productive career.

Once, in a psychology class, a student argued with his professor (there's that dull old prof again) about why any young person should be required to stay in high school. "It's like society bribes us to go to school," he complained. "Why should I have to do what I don't want to do?"

In a way, the young student was right, but the obligation to perform a skill and carry your own weight is just part of what is expected of any adult in any society. The reality is that if you aren't able to carry your own weight, someone else will have to carry you.

Undoubtedly at times, notably when students are not very responsive in class, the professor wonders why society "bribes" *him* to be a teacher!

Bill is likely to be thinking about how great it would be to have a job, be independent and get wheels and a pad. What he isn't thinking about is the disadvantage he will have when he tries to get that job. When he hopes to advance to higher employment levels, most others that he must compete with will have more education than Bill.

Look at it this way... If Billy is willing to take just any job in order to escape from having to go to school, he probably will be able to find one. The problem is that it's likely that that job will quickly become as boring to him as going to school is at the present time. Better, more interesting jobs usually go to those who have more education.

Perhaps, Billy isn't counting on the fact that any job that pays well and is worth having is also wanted by others besides himself. Whether or not he wants to, he will have to compete with others to get any good job. Oh, it's true that he can do the work alright, but so can those others who are applying. Most of those others have finished high school so they will have an edge over him. Bill needs to ask himself honestly why any employer would want to hire the applicant who has the least education, when others, better educated, are available who can do the job just as well as Bill?

The answer, of course, is that most employers won't hire the least educated applicant, so, he is likely to spend much of his life working at less desirable jobs, at lesser salaries and be the one most easily replaced when lay-off time arrives. If he remains on the job, he is likely to be the one passed over at promotion time because he lacks the education enjoyed by most others being considered. Again, why should any employer promote the person who is least qualified if he has several who can do the job and the others are better educated?

The teen-ager who wants desperately to escape from high school is not likely to be looking very far ahead to the times when he will wish that he had stayed in school. He wants his life to be better *now*. To him, better means out of school. It seems appropriate to think about the old German saying, "Ve get too soon oldt undt too late ve get schmart." When Bill is in his thirties, he will be saying to himself, "Sure wish I didn't have to listen *now*, to what I wouldn't listen to when I dropped out..."

Chapter Eleven

Economic Entrapment

Here's another way a person can lose his or her independence and freedom, that is, if that person doesn't think ahead before yielding to temptation. Very few teen-agers have ever thought about this one. It's the kind of loss of control over your life that can happen to you if you give in to too many wants too quickly, wants you can't afford.

A simple story will set the stage for the kind of disappointment that is apt to befall anyone who reaches too far too soon with too little caution. Jennie was just nineteen when she got her first real job, the kind that pays a little more than those minimum wage fast food part-time slave labor jobs that offer no future.

At last, she was making eight bucks an hour, was called an "agent" instead of an employee and was encouraged to dress like a professional woman instead of a uniformed hamburger helper. After two years of part-time slavery, hollaring into a microphone, "Two Whoppers, large fries and one onion rings," Jennie was real excited about getting into the big time. At last she could get her own apartment, buy herself a car and start enjoying life just as God intended. It was nice to be independent. So nice to make her own decisions, buy what she wanted and answer only to herself. It was great for Jennie to be able to treat herself as a grown-up.

The first two apartments Jennie looked at were okay, but were not very impressive. They were quite small, had no dishwasher or garbage disposal and were not in as nice a neighborhood as she had hoped for. Then, she saw the one "to die for." It had lots of extras including a little yard for her puppy.

The rent for the apartment was a little higher than she thought she could afford, but "you only get a first apartment once," she told herself. And besides, she's earning it and so she *deserves* it, right? She just loved the colors in the kitchen. "If I have to, I'll get a roommate to share the rent," she promised herself.

Jennie loves sportscars. There was this one for sale near where she worked that was bright red and had the coolest wheels and a spoiler on the back. Toolin' round in red, cruising with her friends was, like, real bad. *"That's* cool! Cloud nine! The whole nine yards..." The payment would be a bit high, but it would be worth it to have wheels she could count on. You know, when you have a full time job, you need to have dependable transportation, so it's not like you're spending all of your money on something you don't really need. It's true that a somewhat less expensive type of car would have gotten her around, but that wasn't the kind of car she really wanted. "If I'm gonna put out my hard earned money, I ought to get a car I really like," she argued. Besides, "I could probably work in a bit of overtime if I have to," she assured herself. "I just don't want to buy a car that keeps breaking down when I need it," she added.

Jennie was sick of the clothes that mom and dad used to

buy her at Target and at K-Mart. Designer clothes are also to "die for." Those jeans are better made and are on sale and they will let her put them on a charge card so long as she isn't over limit.

Poor Jennie! She had no idea that she was setting herself up for a fall. She had no idea that her long awaited-for opportunity to be fancy free was going to result in the most painful loss of freedom that she could imagine.

You see, Jennie was fooling herself into thinking that she could have what she couldn't afford. It didn't work out as Jennie planned it. Roommates are not very dependable. Just when you think that you can count on them to come up with their share of the expenses for rent, utilities, phone and food, they become unemployed or decide to move in with their boyfriends! Jennie's job wasn't as secure as she thought it would be. Of course, what did turn out to be very dependable was the rent that came due at the first of each month, the car payment that had to be paid and all of those utility bills and credit card payments that were soon overdue. Welcome to adulthood, Jennie!

Do you know what all of this is called? It's *economic entrapment.* It happens when you owe everybody and just can't manage to make your income stretch enough to stay out of trouble. It's when you don't have money for gas for "Bessie" after all of the necessary bills are paid. It's using one credit card to make the payments for the others.

It's a different kind of slavery brought about by your inability to say *"No"* to yourself. At last, Jennie had the opportunity to be free and independent, but she blew it because she was thinking more about the benefits of freedom than she was of the requirement for responsible decision-making. As with so many teen-agers, she wanted too much too soon and just couldn't discipline herself.

Do you know what the worst part was? It was when she finally had to admit to mom and dad that they were right when they warned her that the plush apartment was too expensive, that the car was going to cost too much to repair and that she was using the credit cards way too often. Parents can sure be a pain! Damn it! Why do they have to be so right all of the time?

Economic dependence is a lot like alcohol or drug dependance. It sneaks up on its unsuspecting victims who, while enjoying the benefits, fail to see the threat of the oncoming train. POW! Jennie didn't know what hit her. Tragically, the young lady who wanted so much to be on her own can't recover without the help of others (usually mom and dad).

This would never happen to you, of course, because you know you have to pay for anything you get. Beware! When those credit cards start to come for free in the mail, so also comes the temptation to use them and to overuse them. Things that you wouldn't buy if you had to pay cash for them are within reach if you still have a high enough plastic limit. It's just too tempting to carry goods out of the store now and worry about paying later.

Do you remember the discussion in Chapter One about how the tobacco executives are suckering people into dependence on their products, not caring about whether or not their customers get addicted to nicotine? Well, that's similar to what businesses and banks are doing to people with their enticing offerings of multiple credit cards. It isn't that they want to see people lose control over their spending habits, it's just that they can make enormous amounts of money in interest on lots of these credit card purchases and the more they can get people to buy items on credit, the greater the profits for those in the industry. *They* are the ones who get rich!

The problem is not limited to teen-agers, of course. Many adults find themselves losing their credit and their cars, even their homes because they let their spending habits get out of control. Good money management surely requires a great deal of personal self-discipline. It does require dependable control over personal wants.

Drugs, booze, sex without discipline, the temptation to overspend, all lure the teen-ager to test the limits. "You only live once," some will argue. Hopefully, however, *you* will see the traps. *You* will wisely decide to keep your life under control. Anyone with any sense knows that you can't keep overspending and stay out of trouble!

Have you ever been to a gambling casino? You would be amazed to know the number of people who get addicted to gambling. It's really a blast... It does pay off occasionally. For a very few, it can pay off enormously.

Yet, for most it is a costly enterprise without any prize. The spinning wheels dazzle the eyes with their play, but they rarely pay. Those in the gambling industry know the conditioning power of occasional reinforcement for pulling levers, pushing buttons, spinning wheels and tossing dice. They know that people will put lots of money into the slots and on the tables just to get any slim shot to win.

Hope springs eternal. May the odds be with you... Yet, they seldom are. What is more certain by far is the loss of your money. Occasional reinforcement has a strengthening effect on gambling activities that is so powerful that many people lose control over their play. They become so addicted to the machines, the blackjack tables and the roulette wheel that they can't stay away.

Drinks are free at the casino. *There's* a winning combination! Not for the gamblers, for the casino operators. Alcohol and slim odds. There's a losing combination, for sure. For those who like to drink and play, reality strikes another day. And then, for sure, there's hell to pay.

Chapter Twelve

Getting a Life...

So, you have almost completed your reading of this well-intended little book. You've been preached at, advised at, lectured at and analyzed so much that you're back to where you started. You still don't know if you are being told the truth or if you're being sold a bill of goods. You want to do the right thing, but you don't want to miss out on much of life either. After all, you only go around once, isn't that true?

What matters, however, isn't whether or not you get a go-round. What matters is *how* you go-round. Do you go-round with a little class or do you do it just to do it? Do you develop a nice balanced life-style or do you just flop from one crisis to another, always relying on someone else to bail you out?

Do you become a swearin' smokin' drinkin' druggin' tough guy(or gal) who appears to be rather loose on traditional values so as to impress others with your phoney independence? Do you dedicate yourself to the task of convincing everyone in the world that you are different? Do you see yourself as special, not one of the masses? Do the rules of life seem to apply to everyone else, but not to you? Do you jaywalk or park your car cross-wise?

Of course in this book, it's just been more and more of the same. The same things your teachers and your parents have been saying for years as they told you everything to do. And you' re really tired of hearing it. That "more of the same" translates into "Be a good balanced karate kid. Eat your green vegetables. Stay away from cigarettes, booze and drugs. Get good grades and make mom and dad proud..." No s..; think only pure thoughts.

Yuk!!! What a bummer! Talk about Dullsville...

Let's face a fact of life. If you don't do it that way, you end up living a miserable life. You may feel that it takes guts to be different. And to some extent that's true. However, it's not whether you are different that counts, it's *how* you are different.

Stoned people are different. Drunks are different. So are those who resist all authority, but they don't make much of a contribution to a better life for anyone. Especially for themselves. They spin their wheels, grind their gears, swerve carelessly to the left and right, endangering others along the way. And they get nowhere.

If nowhere is where you want to go, just follow their example. Join the crowd. Light up, drink up, snort, shoot up and join the crowd. You will find lots of company, but you will be lonely. You'll have friends, but they will be temporary. You will have some fun, but most of the time you will be miserable...

The reason for this is that you will lack what is essential for a happy life. You will lack direction. And you will lack the self-discipline necessary to reach out toward a productive future. Others will continue to look upon you as though you never caught on. You never learned that anything worth having must be paid for by careful planning and disciplined effort. Self-discipline is essential.

It's tough to become an adult. It's tougher still to become a self-disciplined, self-sufficient adult. And toughest of all to become a self-disciplined, self-sufficient independent and productive adult. You just can't get to that kind of positive life-style by escaping into self-centered play. Sooner or later, everyone who elects to avoid reality by spending too much of life playing and too little of life setting good goals and working like hell to achieve them will find himself or herself left behind by others.

It's very sad... Some people waste the potential they have. They miss out on so much of life because they find too much fun in escape. Searching for contentment and freedom from stress and anxiety, they turn to substance abuse that leaves them dependent and unhappy.

There is a brighter side to this... One of the truly great things about America is the fact that the majority of its teen-agers have their heads on straight. That's right. They *are* reasonably well-balanced and their heads are squarely on their shoulders. Most kids have straight edges!

Most don't need cigarettes, booze and drugs. Most of America's kids resist premarital sex. Most of them recognize the temptations and know how important it is to avoid them. They know that the cigarette company advertisers are trying to sucker them into contributing to the wealth of the tobacco industry. They know that alcohol abuse can be devastating to families and that drugs can destroy the addicted person's motivation to achieve. If you are like most teen-agers, you know a trap when you see one. You know that what feels good, sometimes isn't.

Some teens don't avoid those traps. Some simply go with the flow. Unsuspecting, innocent and vulnerable, many teen-agers smoke, then wish they didn't have to. Some drink, then wish they could find an easy way to get their habit under control. Then they can't. Some do drugs and wish they hadn't ever started. Some let their sexuality get out of control, resulting in unplanned parenthood. As they mature, they wish they had made some wiser decisions while they were still young. Many adults in their thirties, looking back, find themselves wishing, as the song goes, that they "didn't know now, what they didn't know then."

Wise decisions aren't only for older people. Teens can choose wisely as well. And most of them do. That's the good news. Most teens become very capable grown-ups with good discipline, positive attitudes and promising futures.

Which will it be for *you? Are* you willing to work for a good education? Are you willing to respect authority or must you challenge it? Are you willing to be influenced by those with more experience and a bit more knowledge about how self-discipline pays off in life? Are you able to say "No" to yourself when you should? Most of today's teen-agers are listening... How about *you?*

Chapter Thirteen

At Last! High School is a Done Deal!

For awhile there, You thought that you would never get out.

School is such a drag. It's a bummer that never seems to end. But, now you're seventeen and you are free! Awesome ! Now you can get a job, get your own car, set up your own apartment and start to live without having to answer to anyone. If you want to stay out late, you can. If you want to have friends over, you can. If you want to leave your apartment in a mess, you can. Mom and Dad won't be there to chew you out. Best of all, you can come and go as you like. That's called *freedom!*

Independence – That's what you want. You're tired of being told what to do and when to do it. You're tired of being told what you can't do and you want to make your own decisions. Yeah, you will make some mistakes, but isn't that the way to learn? Problem is, some young people make mistakes that are so serious that they cost lives or do terrible harm to others. If you drink and drive, you could kill someone. Smoking pot while driving can have tragic consequences.

If you don't control your sexual behavior, you could become a parent at a time when you can hardly take care of yourself , let alone a child. If you cannot restrain yourself when it comes time to manage your own budget, you can find yourself in overwhelming debt, and be hounded by bill collectors, even be caught without the rent for the next month.

In order to become an independent adult, you will need to become a producer as well as a consumer. When you were young, your parents provided for your needs and you were a happy consumer. They bought your food and clothes, provided for your school needs and gave you spending money for your trips to the mall. If you are going to become an independent person you will have to earn those things for yourself.

So, you had better think a bit before taking the plunge.

Well, now, let's take a look at what kind of producing you must do in order to set up that longed-for independence. How much income will you need in order to have your own apartment and a car that will get you wherever you want to go and back home again? Let's see – rent will take about $400 a month or so. A car payment, well, about $125 a month, unless Dad gives you his cast-off Toyota with the missing rear window and bald tires (no spare). Figure another $100 per month for car insurance. Utility bills (electric and water) will run about $75 or so, depending on how loud you play your profane rap.

Getting a bit costly, huh? Well, do you suppose you will have to buy food also? Another $100 per month? What about gas for that car?

No use havin' it if you can't drive it. Right? Pray that it keeps on going.

Of course, you can give up a little of the independence by dropping by to see Mom and Dad several times a week, during mealtime. That's a savings. No more stops at Starbuck's for that latte' that's to die for.

And what about clothes? You know, like in designer jeans with ragged holes at the knees. And awesome lookin' shoes... Wouldn't be caught dead at Walmart, huh? Well, that's gotta change, because you will soon learn that you can't afford J C Penney's or Dillard's, not if you want to show your independence by paying your other bills as they come due.

Then, there's the dreaded CCE disease. It catches up with a lot of young people trying to do too much too quickly. They find themselves in a whole heap of trouble. Then it can become impossible to avoid having to go back to their parents for an embarrassing "I told you so" session.

CCE stands for credit card entrapment. Just pay for what you want, using your credit card. When you don't have enough available money to make your payment, just take out more on another card.

When you don't know whether or not you can afford to buy something, just reach into your purse or wallet for the Visa card. No problem...

YOU MUST LIMIT YOUR SPENDING. If you want to become financially independent, you must limit your outgo to what you have earned, rather than what you want. God, what an awful rule... You've got to get a job that pays well and you need to spend less than what that job brings in. *That's* the key to a life of independence. "But, most jobs don't pay that much," you say. "How can I get a job that will cover the cost of my apartment, a car payment, car insurance, food, clothes, etc., especially, when I have to start out with no real employment experience?"

Believe it or not, there is an answer to this unfortunate dilemma, one that makes more sense than searching for a rich person to marry.

It involves putting that entry into independence off for awhile while you get training beyond high school that is likely to increase your value to an employer. Maybe a two-year or even a four-year college degree.

"But, I'm so sick of school," you say. That's a perfectly normal reaction. You want to get out into the real world, where the excitement is. Good for you! But the real world can kick the Hell out of you if you are not prepared for it. And the more education you have, the better prepared for it you will be.

So old professor Huard is telling you about a way to become quite independent that isn't easy, but it is more likely to pay off in the long run. Maybe Mom and Dad would be willing to help you for a few more years if you decided to go to college. If you continue to live at home, it will mean that you will still be under their very restricive rules when you feel you are ready to live by your own. However, you can live by your own rules when you can afford to pay your own way. When you can, your parents will be very, very proud of you. Your independence will be your hard-earned, well-deserved reward.

Chapter Fourteen

Is It Harder for Teen-agers Today?

Well now, so you think that's true, huh? What with pot and meth and drugs like ecstacy that older generations did not have tempting them into trouble, Grandpa and Grandma had it easier than you do today. Is that the way you see it? And what about all of the T V sex and internet porn so readily available today? Don't those temptations make it a lot tougher to be a straight up kid these days? Aren't more things expected of the kids today? Didn't Mom and Dad have it much easier than the young high school and junior college age kids of today? Today, you can't even get a decent job unless you've got two years of college.

And there's Mom and Dad, always on your back about something.

Get better grades in school, don't carouse around at night, be careful who your friends are, keep your room clean, don't have sex. Don't even think for yourself. They still want to treat you like a kid. Can't parents see that by the time you are sixteen or seventeen you need to be treated as an adult?

After all, you can drive a car. You can go shopping by yourself or with your friends. You should be allowed to decide what you can wear, how late you can stay out at night and who you want to run around with. You are old enough to judge for yourself what you can and cannot do. "I'll sure be glad when I can make my own decisions instead of always being told what to do, when I can be free instead of always being controlled. It's different today than the way it was when Grandma and Grandpa and Mom and Dad were our age..."

That's quite true, of course. It's not the same. But don't just assume that that means it was a whole lot easier being young then as compared to now. Let your old college professor give you his memory of being young "When I was sixteen I was in love. Just as in love as any of you young folks get today. And as I look back on it now, I realize that I knew about as much about love and marriage and responsibility toward the opposite sex as you do today – just about nothing at all.

All I knew was that being in love could be wonderful and downright awful at the same time. I have in the past described being in love as like riding your tricycle down the basement stairs, quite a thrill, but with uncertain consequences. Was I mature enough at, say, seventeen or eighteen to decide if I should move in with my "significant" other?

No way... And that's true today, just as it was when I was that age." "Oh, Grandpa," the kids say, "you're so old-fashioned, young people do that all of the time nowadays." "Yes they do," Grandpa says, "and they get into a whole heap o' trouble as a result nowadays – more often than ever before."

Was it easier for Grandpa to be young in his time than it is for young folks today? If you are nineteen today, you have your own car, a comfy bed to sleep in at night, good available meals and parents who will respond to help you with any problem you might have if you simply dial them on your handy cellphone.

That doesn't make being young easy for you, but let's compare that with what nineteen year-old fellows had to deal with a couple of generations ago. See if you think that it was easier for Grandpa and others of his generation.

"I well remember," Grandpa says, "the afternoon when I came home from my job as a washing machine repairman (or boy) to find a long official-looking white envelope waiting for me.

Mom knew what the letter was. I was just fascinated by the official seal over the return address. "From the office of the President of the United States." "Greetings, Mr. Donald Huard," the letter inside said, "You have been selected by a committee of your peers to serve in the armed forces of the United States of America. You are hereby instructed to appear at 101 N. Second Street in Phoenix, Arizona at 7:00 A M on November 28th 1952 for induction into The United States Army." Grandpa noted that he was nineteen years old at the time.

"There was no "Would you like to join?" No "What branch would you like?" No nuthin', just be there! Or else… On that morning I lost my comfy bed at home, the use of my car, my freedom to go to the McDonald's for a burger when I wanted to and dates with my sweetheart. I was denied any choice as to whether or not I wanted to go to college. I spent the next sixteen weeks running up and down the hills of Fort Ord in northern California, a thousand miles from my mommy and daddy as I learned how to be an infantryman.

Still, I considered myself lucky as I was assigned to an

engineering outfit serving in Alaska. Eventually, I became an aircraft mechanic, feeling most fortunate that I didn't have to go to Korea where over 38,000 young soldiers died in the service of their country. Many of them were just teen-agers."

Is it tougher to be young person today than it was in those earlier generations? Your professor just cannot buy it. The directions that you go as you enter your twenties will be largely up to you. The choices are yours. You will make the decisions that affect your life. In earlier times that was not always the case. It has always been challenging to be a responsible young adult. There is no indication that it is any tougher now than it was in earlier times. If anything, just the reverse is true.

Young folks have advantages and opportunities far greater than those available to young adults in generations passed. You are on wheels rather than on foot. You frequently eat in nearby restaurants, something your grand parents could rarely do. Most of you have affordable community colleges in your own areas.

Perhaps your greater freedoms have resulted in some greater temptations, but that doesn't mean that times are tougher for you.

Let's see how smart you are. Let's see how effectively you can resist those temptations to be dumb and to get yourself in dumb trouble. You know what Grandpa means. Dumb like in getting involved with drugs or alcohol. Dumb like in being an angry, aggressive, careless driver. Dumb like in starting to smoke, thinking that it makes you seem more grown-up when actually, it just makes you gross. Dumb is when "fitting in" with your friends is more important than using good common sense. Being dumb is what you regret years later when when you should have listened to your parents and you didn't.

A really smart teen-ager makes really smart decisions along the way. A wise teen-ager drives his (or her) car with respect for others and the speed limits. A wise teen-ager has some life OFF of his (or her) cellphone. A wise teen-ager is able to say "No" to himself (or herself) even with a credit card in hand. A wise teen-ager often says, "Thanks Mom, thanks Dad. I love you."

Chapter Fifteen

Becoming Independent

Jenny wants Mom and Dad to accept the fact that she has grown up and no longer needs to be treated as if she were still a child. She wants to get an apartment, drive her own car and be free to make her own decisions about picking her own friends, deciding for herself where she should go and when she needs to be back at home at night. She's very tired of being told what she should do and why some things are not wise to do. After all, she's eighteen now and that means she's an adult.

Or, at least she thinks she is. But, is she really? Parents know that a person becomes an adult when he or she beomes self-sufficient, that is, no longer dependent on others to meet one's own needs. If independence from her parents is what Jenny wants, she has to get a job that provides enough income to cover the expenses for all of the nice things she desires.

"Oh, I know," she will say, but there is a difference between knowing and doing, i.e., a difference between needing a good job and actually getting one.

If Jenny has become a successful high school graduate, she's much more likely to get that kind of job. A community college degree would increases her chances even more. A four-year college or University degree could set the stage for a very meaningful career.

However, more boring classroom attendance and studying may be the farthest thing from Jenny's mind. She may be sick of school and feel that she is ready for the work-a-day world.

She probably feels that she is ready to reach out, to explore the opportunities, to meet the challenges on her own.

Jenny's parents want her to succeed. They wish her well, love her very much and try to be supportive and caring as the transition from childhood to adulthood takes place. Jenny will soon learn that it isn't as easy as she thought it would be. She will eventually learn that it's necessary to compete with other applicants to get any job that can pay for the things she wants.

Oh, it's true that there are lots of low paying fast food jobs Available, like flippin' burgers or cleaning off tables. But they are minimum wage jobs that don't pay enough to cover even any apartment rent, let alone a car payment, the cellphone bill the TV cable bill and food for herself and her little dog.

Sounds depressing, doesn't it? How does Jenny get a good job when the interviewers keep asking her if she finished high school or if she has a college degree? What about experience?

How does she get experience if no one will give her a good job to begin with? If there is any answer, it's in accepting a lower level beginning job and being patient about going out on her own before she is ready. That probably means continued help from Mom and Dad.

The best approach is the least desired one for many high school graduates. It involves accepting parental help if it is still available, remaining at home and going on to the community college. Some parents can afford to send their kids to a fine University, even an expensive one, but many cannot. A local community college is usually a good choice.

The available degree is a two-year Associate in Arts degree. While not considered as a "professional" degree, in a period of just four full semesters it can provide training in a very wide variety of areas. Jenny can become a secretary, a receptonist, a dental assistant, a medical records clerk, a cosmotologist, a computer technician a criminal justice trainee, a practical nurse just to mention a few options.

Then there are programs in the arts including music, dance, and theater. Many of the programs are considered as preparatory for University training in the professions of education, business, science, etc. Jenny would be wise to stop by the admitting office to pick up a free college catalog to learn about the available study options.

But, why the emphasis on more education? Is it really that Important? Well, no... Not if a young person is to remain satisfied with a low paying job with little opportunity for any advancement and a better salary. It's important only if there are dreams of a better future. A good future doesn't happen by chance - not usually. Hard work, good planning and strong self-discipline set the stage for a good future.

Consider it *this* way. Imagine yourself *not* as a young person looking for a good job, but instead as a personnel man or woman looking for a good qualitfied person to hire as a new employee. You can choose any one of your applicants, all of whom want the job. Which one would you choose? Would you choose the one with the least education? Would you hire the one with the least training or experience?

That's not likely, of course. Bosses want the most qualified people on their teams.

What that means is that as a prospective employee Jenny will find herself in competition with others applying for any job that is worth having. If her education, training, any disciplined skills and motivation are not as strong as those of some other applicants, she will not get the job. A more qualified applicant will. That's the simple reason for encouraging Jenny to go on for more schooling. It's a high price to pay, but those who pay the price end up in a better position to get the better jobs. When you think about it, isn't that the way it should be? Shouldn't the rewards go to those who have worked the hardest to get them?

"But, I don't know what I want to do," Jenny is likely to complain, using it as an excuse for not going on to the community college. She may not be aware that most beginning students don't know that either. Only as they take their varied classes will they become familiar with the many opportunities available to them.

Some classes will be more interesting than others. Some professors will influence Jenny's thinking more than others. If she works hard and gets reasonably good grades, she will gain confidence and be encouraged to continue. That's the process that often results in the development of a career. Many young people will go week after week, month after month and even year after year avoiding the opportunities that college can offer. Unwilling to pay the price, they are much less likely to move toward the independence they crave. Does Jenny want to remain dependent on others or does she really want to earn her own way to the self-sufficient lifestyle of an adult?

Jenny should think seriously about her future...

Author's Note...

Did you like this little book? Was it worth the time it took to read it? I surely hope so. You see, I don't like seeing your friends screwing up their lives by letting substances like pot, meth or booze get their awful hooks into them. I'm really convinced that teen-agers can get into a lot of trouble with "safe" sex that isn't.

Do you agree? There are many who do not, of course, but do *you* agree? If you do, then just give your copy of this little book to a friend and tell him or her that you thought it was interesting.

Most little books like this end up on a shelf in a corner where they are ignored for years. They collect dust. You won't let that happen to your copy, will you?

Do you have a boyfriend or girlfriend who is starting to smoke and you wish he or she wouldn't? Maybe someone is boozing it up too much. Is a friend of yours fooling around with pot, meth (or sex) and are you afraid that he (she) is on the road to entrapment?

Don't just toss this book aside. Give it to someone you care about. *You* are a good kid. You mean well. Let's join together and make a difference...